GOD'S HISTORY

By
ROLF RENDTORFF

GOD'S HISTORY

A Way Through the Old Testament

Translated by
GORDON C. WINSOR

THE WESTMINSTER PRESS
Philadelphia

Translation of *Gottes Geschichte,* by Rolf
Rendtorff
© Furche-Verlag H. Rennebach KG., Hamburg
1962

STANDARD BOOK NO. 664-24852-7

LIBRARY OF CONGRESS CATALOG CARD NO. 69-18648

Published by The Westminster Press®
Philadelphia, Pennsylvania

PRINTED IN THE UNITED STATES OF AMERICA

Contents

TRANSLATOR'S PREFACE

The reader may well ask what possible excuse there might be for offering the layman yet another book on the Old Testament. Indeed, there are many volumes available describing the myriad details of Israel's history, complete with names, battles, dates, and the difficult problems about the vast literature that tells the story. But Professor Rendtorff has written a very different sort of book.

The central purpose of this work is found in its treatment of the traditions of Israel. For Rendtorff, GOD's HISTORY, as his title aptly puts it, is not simply the history of Israel, but rather the traditions about that history. These traditions are seen as created out of the historical experiences of Israel and as the creators of further experience. Most importantly, he shows that these ancient traditions reflect on the part of their transmitters the firm belief that Israel had met with a God who was directing the destiny of Israel and of the entire world, and that the traditions are, in a very real sense, God's history. And further, he emphasizes the substantial impact that these traditions have had on the civilizations of the Christian West. Thus, these traditions are yet living and worthy of continued study by the modern man.

One may be pardoned for asking what is so important about all this. For, on the surface, it appears to be very similar to much that has been seen in print previously about God's acting in history. But Rendtorff's discussion contains some significant contributions to a complicated problem that has troubled theologians for many years. Just how important to the Christian faith is history, and what is the relationship of the individual's faith to that history? The varied answers that theologians have offered are confusing, not to say disheartening, to the average layman.

Let us examine the issue more closely. Traditionally, it had been held that the Biblical accounts were all straightforward stories telling quite literally what events transpired, what God had said to men, and what they had said to each other. The believer had simply to accept the stories as firsthand history. But the studies of generations of devoted scholars have shown that these stories cannot be understood so easily—that there were many literary forms developed out of variant traditions, and that there was a difference between "what actually happened" and what the tradition told about it.

Now, granted that such a difference exists, what does one make of it? The answer to this question, posed by inquiring laymen as well as scholars, is what is presently plaguing the world of Biblical scholarship. The famous Swiss theologian, Karl Barth, attempted a solution by turning attention away from historical problems and pointing to Christ as the sole source of revelation. In the case of the Old Testament, this meant seeing it solely in terms of its ability to point forward to the coming of Christ. This Christocentric view has undeniable attractiveness and great power. But it has never been able to deal adequately with Old Testament history, for the period of time prior to Christ has no real revelatory function here. Yet, as Rendtorff argues, Christ himself and the New Testament writers present a message clearly based on the Old Testament as an authoritative work involving more than just predictions of the coming of the Messiah. Surely, to be fair to Christ and to the New Testament requires that we take seriously the Old Testament as well.

A different kind of solution has been offered by a group of

scholars who use the German term *Heilsgeschichte* as a key. Its meaning is the "history of salvation." They make the claim that at certain critical times in Israel's history, such as the exodus and the taking of Canaan, God acted and thereby revealed himself. By centering faith on the events themselves, the difficulties of the Biblical texts can be relegated safely to the area of critical studies. This is also an attractive solution, for it allows the student complete freedom in understanding the creation of the Biblical texts by processes of storytelling and legend-making. But the main interest is in the events themselves, and therefore study is directed toward a more exact knowledge of the events behind the texts. This, too, has a genuine attractiveness, for history is the stuff of life: real and concrete. It beckons the student to use his archaeological and historical tools to discover the hand of God in the past and thus to expect God's hand in the present.

But, alas, there are difficulties here as well. Which events are to be judged important enough to bear God's revelation? What criterion shall be used to discriminate between revelatory and nonrevelatory events? Any answer will prove to be distressingly subjective in nature. What is worse, historical tools do not prove to be very adept at discovering God's hand in anything. The secular historian will find his discussion of the materials of Israel's history revolving around sizes of armies, geography, and economic conditions, while the theologian is having a hard time arguing that any particular event was shaped by God's intervention.

A way out of this dilemma has been suggested by still another group of Biblical scholars—those following the lead of the great German New Testament student, Rudolf Bultmann. His position is that revelation takes place not so much in the historical act itself as in the heart of the person confronted by the event. Thus one is to see the Biblical story as its writers' expression of faith in the face of events. No matter how much that story is told in unbelievably miraculous terms, the point is their faith reflected in the telling, and, in turn, our faithful response. Our attention is therefore directed away from history itself (which can never be recovered anyway, according to Bultmann) and toward our own affirmation that we are becoming genuine persons *now* as we are confronted by God. Bultmann has summed up his view in writing to a group of English laymen by saying that the message of the Bible is to help the believer to know that "God is *my* God."

Again, we have a position that has satisfied many people with its elimination of all problems of the miraculous and with its concentration on individual Christian faith. Yet, for many there remains a great difficulty. This is that there must have been something in the actual events of Biblical history which inspired faith in the original tellers and writers of the story. The Bible seems to take its own story quite seriously.

The foregoing paragraphs have indicated, in a very brief space, something of the labors of Biblical scholars over the past several generations in trying to speak to the question of history, tradition, and faith. The picture has been considerably simplified, and those who wish more detailed enlightenment on these positions and others will do well to read Carl Braaten's excellent but difficult *History and Hermeneutics* (Vol. II of New Directions in Theology Today; The Westminster Press). But our purpose here has been to provide a background against which Professor Rendtorff's book may be properly appreciated. For it is part of a significant new theological movement trying out a new approach to the same issues the others have addressed. This movement is associated largely with the name of Wolfhart Pannenberg, a young German theologian.

The major theme here is that history *is* revelation. Not that it *contains* revelation, but that it *is* revelation. But the revelation cannot be fully understood from within history; understanding can come only at the end of history—which we cannot see. However, Christ is the revelation of God's final purpose, coming in the midst of that history. Thus, the promises of blessing and guidance, received at early stages of Israel's history, point toward an end to be consummated in Christ.

The Biblical story is not identical with the history, either as it looks back to the events of the past or ahead to the end, but, nevertheless, it is a tradition reflecting Israel's experience with the promises and its expectations for the future. Furthermore, the tradition is itself a part of Israel's history and plays a role in the shaping of the history. Thus, history and tradition, both taken seriously, are seen to be inseparable.

Rendtorff's purpose in the present book is to detail for the average reader how this viewpoint works out in studying the Old Testament. There is no need to review the book's contents here, as he writes with clarity and without burdensome technical detail. Suffice it to say that he surveys the major elements and stages of the Biblical traditions as they reflect Israel's past and establish a basis for faithful living in the face of ever new crises in the future, including our own.

One may, of course, ask just how successful Rendtorff's efforts are. We have seen that no scholarly views are ever beyond criticism; Pannenberg, Rendtorff, and the others who share this outlook will probably be subjected to the same sort of questioning other Biblical scholars have experienced. But let the reader not be disillusioned by the prospect, for not only is this book part of an important new trend likely to become more prominent, but it is also true that the continuing examination of the Bible's traditions provides for the Christian a way of making them ever fresh and relevant to the issues of his own time. This function is admirably accomplished by Professor Rendtorff.

GOD'S HISTORY

CHAPTER

1

The Origins of the People of Israel

The Old Testament is a controversial book. Not only do the
opponents of the Christian church frequently direct their attacks against the Old Testament, seeking thereby to strike the
church at its roots, but even among people who take a positive stance toward the church or who even consciously regard
themselves as Christians there are many for whom the Old
Testament remains a very problematic book. There have even
been from time to time notable Christian theologians who
have been unwilling to recognize the Old Testament as a constituent part of the Christian Bible. This rejection of the Old
Testament has many grounds. But we shall not pursue them
here; rather, we shall inquire what positive meaning the Old
Testament has for us as Christians today, and why the Christian church cannot renounce this book.

How did it actually happen that the Old Testament came to
be a constituent part of the Christian Bible? This question offers in the first instance a very simple answer: As the Christian
fellowship developed, the Old Testament was there as a holy
book of long standing; it was already in itself, as we would
put it, the "Bible," that is to say, the holy scripture of the Jewish people. And the first Christian community was made up
exclusively of Jews, thus of people for whom the Old Testament was the Bible. Then, in the course of a few decades, a
number of Christian writings appeared, which then gradually

15

came together to form the small book that we call the New Testament. Thus, just as in our Bibles the New Testament follows after the Old, so also the Old Testament existed first, followed much later by the New Testament.

But why, then, did the Christian church retain the Old Testament, having as it did its own collection of holy writings, its New Testament? Would it not have been much more proper to put the New Testament in place of the Old instead of simply attaching the New to the Old? That the Christians of the first centuries did not do this is the more remarkable when one recalls that the Jews never stopped regarding the Old Testament as their Bible, and that for a long time deep enmity reigned between Christians and Jews. Would it not have been much simpler to leave the Old Testament to the Jews and to base the Christian faith wholly on the New Testament?

The Christian church did not do this, and it could not do it lest it depart from the ground on which it stood. Without the Old Testament, the crucial fact of the Christian faith, Christ himself, would have become completely incomprehensible. "Christ" means "the anointed." And this is precisely what the Hebrew or Aramaic "Messiah" means. Christ is the Messiah. But what that means—that Jesus of Nazareth is the Messiah—can be understood only when one knows the Old Testament. For the expectation of the Messiah was indeed an important element of the proclamation of the Old Testament prophets and played an important role among the Jews in the troubled centuries prior to the appearance of Jesus. One certainly could not preach Christ without speaking of this Old Testament expectation.

And there is yet more: When Jesus spoke of God, he had no need of explaining to his listeners which God he meant. Indeed, in the world in which Jesus and his contemporaries lived, men held belief in many gods. But in spite of this, Jesus' hearers certainly did not come to think that he could have meant any other than the God they had heard of and read about, the God of whom the Old Testament spoke. It is completely obvious for the New Testament that, whenever God is spoken of, the God of the Old Testament is meant. And the decisive fact of the Christian proclamation was precisely that this God, who had so often given promises to his people through the long centuries of their history, had now fulfilled them—and how could one speak of that without the Old Testament? For this reason, the apostle Paul, before he could speak of Christ to the Gentiles who did not know the Old Testament, always had to begin by speaking of the promises of God to the Israelite people.

The Christian church is thus rooted deeply in the Old Testament. Were one to attempt to understand the church in such a way as to cut off its roots, it would of necessity wither away. When we speak of the Old Testament, we are at the same time speaking of the roots of the Christian church and the Christian faith. Whether we understand the Old Testament rightly is a question of great significance for every Christian. But we must go yet another step: The world in which we live today, our civilized, modern world, has been built on the foundations of the Christian tradition; even if it appears to be living today without further reliance on this foundation, there can be no doubt that without it the world would not have developed to its present-day form. But the Old Testament is an indispensable part of this foundation; in it the whole Western tradition has one of its most important sources.

Thus we as Christians stand in a deeply historical connection with the Old Testament. For this reason we shall now direct our attention primarily to the history which, so to speak, constitutes the beginning of our own history—the history of the people of Israel, which found its outcome in the Old Testament. And we shall pay attention to the distinctiveness of this history and ask ourselves whether and how far we might recognize therein the roots of our own history even today. If we succeed in this, we shall have learned again to understand the Old Testament's own essential significance.

When one inquires after the beginning of a people's history, in very few cases will one receive an answer that would satisfy a modern historian. Most peoples become conscious of their own history only after they have existed a long time as a people. It is otherwise only in exceptional cases, such as in the development of the American people, which came about in the bright light of history.

The origins of Israel's history also lie in darkness before the inquiring glance of the historian. Yet he does find certain fixed points from which he can orient himself. A particularly characteristic point in the historical tradition of the Old Testament is the awareness of the people of Israel that they had not originally lived in their own land, but had acquired it later. Only after God had led them into the land that he had promised the fathers did they find a homeland. Thus, at first there was a life without a permanent dwelling place, much the same as led by the Bedouin in the lands of the Near East even today. However, many traditions have become fixed in Israel as a result of this period; indeed, this time is, in the consciousness of the people, the decisive and basic time of its history. There are several major groups of traditions in which these memories were fixed.

A first group of traditions speaks of the great figures of the patriarchs Abraham, Isaac, and Jacob. Their manner of living is portrayed after the fashion of the Bedouin. They live in tents as herdsmen and cattle breeders, without fixed dwellings. They have no land belonging to them; instead, they migrate from one place to another. And all manner of events are reported which represent a danger to their existence, yet out of which ever and again they come forth safely. The stories of the patriarchs function as popular folk tales passed on by their descendants from generation to generation. But why were they passed on, ultimately to form a constituent part of the holy scriptures of the people of Israel?

It was certainly not for the reason that the patriarchs had been ideal figures who could serve the people as models to imitate. One cannot assert of any one of the fathers, according to the picture offered by the tradition, that he had always been faultless. Even Abraham, who is portrayed as the father of the faith, is yet shown as a doubter, who, during his sojourn in Egypt, preferred to risk that his wife Sarah might be taken into Pharaoh's harem rather than put himself in danger. A similar thing is told of Isaac, and Jacob is certainly no exemplary figure. On the contrary, along the route of Jacob's life stand the fraud by which he took to himself the birthright and certain not wholly unobjectionable business methods by which he came to power. All this is set forth unsparingly and not varnished over. But for the Biblical accounts these human entanglements and shortcomings do not stand in the forefront. They are a reality dealt with quite soberly, but in the final analysis they do not determine the course of events.

When we read the patriarchal stories as a whole, it becomes obvious that one theme runs throughout like a single red thread: the guidance and blessing of God. The beginning of the story of Abraham shows this: "Now the LORD said to Abram, 'Go from your country and your kindred and your father's house to the land that I will show you'" (Gen. 12:1). The promise of God's guidance stands in the midst of uncertainty at the beginning of this historical process. And throughout the story of the fathers it is shown time and time again how even in the most difficult and apparently hopeless situations the guidance of God finally determines the outcome. At the end of the story of Joseph the matter is summed up: "You meant evil against me; but God meant it for good" (Gen. 50:20). Therein is the story of Joseph and his brethren summarized, and at the same time a criterion established by which all the preceding accounts are to be understood.

Yet a second motive is joined to that of guidance: the blessing. "And I will make of you a great nation, and I will bless you and make your name great." (Gen. 12:2.) God not only led the fathers, but he richly blessed them, so that out of the one whom God's command drew forth from his country a

great people came into being. We can now clearly recognize
why Israel continued to hand on these stories, and why it
did so, right from the beginning of the history of this people.
It was shown in that history that the formation of the people
was a consequence of the divine blessing which had come to
the patriarchs; the whole existence of the people was thus
understood as derived throughout from the blessing of God.

And finally a third motive: "In you all the families of the
earth will be blessed," it is stated in Gen. 12:3 (margin). This
is a particularly significant sentence. In it is expressed the con-
viction that all that has happened to Abraham and Israel is
intended as a blessing for all peoples. What does that mean?
How did this small, insignificant people come to the point of
speaking of its role among the world of nations in this way? It
is faith in the election of Israel that we encounter here. God
acts concerning Israel in a wholly special manner: he has
chosen Israel out of the great multitude of peoples in order
to give it a share in his blessing and his guidance, and he has
thereby assigned Israel a decisive significance for all peoples.
The word "election" often has for us an unpleasant connota-
tion. We associate with it something of self-satisfaction and ar-
rogance. But the account of the election of Abraham does not
give us the slightest excuse for thinking in these terms. Never
is it said that Israel brought forward any kind of presupposition for this election. It was not better than other peoples,
and it had always realized that as a small nation it had slight
political significance. And above all, what then is the meaning of this election? It is certainly not simply precedence and
privilege; rather, it means that the whole burden of responsibility for all mankind falls on this people. Indeed, Israel is not
expected to change the world by its own power; rather, it is
placed on a course wherein God will lead it. But this way is a
way for all mankind: "In you all the families of the earth will
be blessed."

A complacent self-satisfaction with the received blessing is
refuted out of hand. The Old Testament shows how Israel

had ever and again become aware of this responsibility. But at the same time, this responsibility contains the possibility of failure. For Israel was not to be an involuntary instrument of God's plans; rather, it was constantly required to go in this way consciously and in ever new recognition of its responsibility. And it often failed. The prophets had held this failure up before it time after time and had proclaimed God's judgment on it. And this judgment received its full weight and depth by virtue of the fact that it was precisely the chosen people who had been struck by it. But yet again, election was the reason why God never allowed this people to be completely overthrown. God's faithfulness to his choice allowed Israel to endure even through his judgment.

If we look back today, some three thousand years after these words about the beginning of the patriarchal history had been written, we see that they have been fulfilled in a peculiar way. In the world of the Near East there were, in the time of the fathers of Israel, great and glittering religions. In particular, in Egypt and Babylonia there flourished the cult of many gods who were worshiped there in a scarcely imaginable way. In comparison, the Bedouin religion of the fathers of Israel must have appeared completely ridiculous. However, the great religions of Egypt and Babylonia disappeared. Only in recent times has the work of scholars brought them to light again in little fragments. Their gods remain dead and no one prays to them any longer. But the religion of Israel lives. The God of Israel's fathers made himself known as the one, true God, and through the Christian tradition he has become known throughout the whole world. We are scarcely aware any longer of the foregone conclusion with which we customarily speak of God as the one God and thereby have taken up the fundamental element of the Israelite religion.

Thus the origin of the people of Israel was in fact an event that has come to hold the greatest significance for all humanity. The decisive fact therein is the religion of Israel, its recognition of the one, true God. But this religion is not to be

separated from the national existence of Israel. For God has
revealed himself in this way and in no other: in the midst of
the history of a particular people, in inseparable connection
with its destiny. We cannot actually speak of God, of the one,
true God, without bearing in mind this beginning of the history of his revelation. God has revealed himself to mankind,
in the first instance, as the God of Israel.

For Israel how intimately the revelation of God was bound
up with the history of the people is shown particularly clearly
in the second great group of traditions out of the early times
of Israel. In this group is told how the Israelites, driven by
famine, were drawn to Egypt, where the vegetation is not dependent on the vagaries of rainfall, but where the survival of
the inhabitants is based on the overflow of the Nile River even
in dry years. In Egypt, the Israelites were drawn into forced
labor by the then-reigning Pharaoh and severely oppressed.
Yet they were able finally to escape out of this slavery. The
Egyptians pursued them, but the Israelites were saved in a
marvelous way: they passed with dry feet through an arm of a
sea whose water then suddenly flowed back so that the pur-
suing Egyptians were completely destroyed by it.

This event has been honored and celebrated in Israel again
and again as God's great act of salvation. It formed the basis
of the Israelite confession of faith, as it comes to expression at
the beginning of the Ten Commandments: "I am the LORD
your God, who brought you out of the land of Egypt, out of
the house of bondage" (Ex. 20:2), or, as it is put more than
once in other places: "The LORD brought us out of Egypt with
a mighty hand and an outstretched arm, with great terror,
with signs and wonders." Thus, it was no merely spiritual revelation which furnished Israel with the foundation of its
faith; rather, wholly concrete experiences gave it the certainty that God was with Israel. Israel had experienced God
as the God of history. He acted in historical events and in
them revealed himself. Israel knew him because his acts had
been experienced. This recognition of God as the Lord of his-

tory stands for us also at the beginning of the history of his revelation.

But if we would fully understand the experiences that Israel had had with the acts of God in history, then we must note another important point: beginning with the patriarchal story, and afterward again and again, God had given the fathers a promise of guidance and blessing, numerous descendants, and, finally, the possession of the land—all of that was promised the fathers. And even in the accounts of the rescue from Egypt the promise has a significant meaning; namely, that God called Moses and announced to him that through him he would bring the people out of Egyptian bondage. Thus the historical action of God was announced beforehand in the word of promise; and when it then occurred, Israel experienced at the same time the fulfillment of the promise that God had given.

Israel thus saw its history from the beginning as a movement from the promise on through to its fulfillment. God gave himself to be recognized precisely in that he fulfilled his promises in his historical actions: "You shall know that I am the LORD your God, who has brought you out from under the burdens of the Egyptians" (Ex. 6:7). And, not only at the beginning, but also as time went on, Israel experienced again and again how the promise was fulfilled and how new promises directed its view again to the future. Israel's history did not travel in a straight line and without disturbance, but it constantly pointed to the future; it was always history under the promise. And when the early Christian congregations spoke of the fulfillment of all promises in Jesus Christ, they had thereby taken up this understanding of history which from the beginning had propelled Israel.

In yet a third group of traditions Israel articulated its early encounters with God. This group told how God had appeared to his people on Mt. Sinai and had there concluded a covenant with them. Through the establishment of this covenant Israel knew itself from the beginning of its history to be in a close

relationship with God. Once more there is expressed here
the idea of the election of Israel. For this covenant association had its origin, not in a decision of the people to honor
this God, but rather in a decision of God to make this people
his: "You shall be my own possession among all peoples" (Ex.
19:5). And therefore the continuance of this covenant was not
dependent on whether Israel remained true to it; God himself
was the guarantee, his faithfulness was the basis on which it
rested.

But that did not mean that the conduct of the people itself
was thereby completely immaterial. Quite the contrary! God
had announced his will to the people in the making of the
covenant, and they were now to live according to that will.
Thus the covenant was indeed the free gift of God to Israel,
but at the same time it contained the requirement that Israel live wholly according to God's will. The Ten Commandments were the summation of this will of God, the covenant
regulation, to which Israel was bound. Here again an important thrust of the Israelite religion comes to expression, a
thrust that has retained its unlimited importance for us. The
honoring of God is not accomplished solely, and never, in the
first instance, in that which we term "divine worship," thus in
religious, cultic arrangements. Much more, God demands at
the same time and above all a quite definite association of
humanity in the world in which God has placed it—in the
family and in relationship to the neighbor within the society
in which we live. The Ten Commandments, which belong to
the oldest religious traditions of Israel, have for us even today
a binding power.

Thus the oldest traditions of Israel show to what high de-
gree during the origin of this people perceptions have come to
light that have become for us today the indispensable foundation of Christianity and of human life. The history of Israel
is our history, on the basis of which we live today. And this is
precisely what we can learn from Israel: to live on the basis
of history. For that is the elementary thrust of Israelite reli-

gion, which has maintained itself through the course of the centuries. Not simply to live in history! And this we can learn from the Old Testament: the passionate interest in that which has happened, which means the endeavor to understand what has happened, and the deep consciousness of an inescapable responsibility toward history. But all this does not have its roots in the present. It springs from the knowledge that that which is now occurring is inseparably connected with what has already happened, that it springs out of the past, which is not dead and done with, but is a living, decisive part of the present.

However, to live on the basis of history does not mean living in the past. It means, rather, on the one hand, living toward the future—as is shown in Israelite thought in the movement from promise to fulfillment. But it also means, on the other hand, living in the present. Historical thought was never for Israel a flight from the present, whether toward the past or the future. The question about history is finally decided by the question about the particular position in this history. It is therefore necessary to understand the particular present on the basis of the historical context.

Many readers will perhaps now be concerned with the question as to whether all that is told us in the Old Testament is really true. When we speak today of the "controversial Bible," there are most generally such questions in the foreground as are dealt with somewhat sensationally under the title "The Bible was right after all." But through these questions we allow ourselves all too readily to conceal from view the important assertions of the Old Testament. Without doubt, the old traditions of Israel contain many historically valuable statements. There was a time in Old Testament studies when there was too much skepticism concerning its historical foundations. The archaeological investigation of the last century has brought us valuable disclosures and helped us to see many things in a new light. But at the same time these texts are not documentary accounts giving us direct views of the events

themselves. Between the lives of the patriarchs and the record-
ing of the stories in their present form lie centuries in which
these accounts were told again and again, certainly being
much altered in the process. Thus it is that, for the historian,
many questions remain which can be only partially answered. Others he must leave unanswered if he would be completely honest.

But the constant repetition of the stories has led precisely
to the result that the decisive features, fundamental to the
faith of Israel, have come through ever more clearly. And for
this reason, these texts are for us historical documents of the
highest value. They show us how God had led Israel in its
history, and how, as a result of its divine guidance, this people had understood its history. These are two sides of the same
fact which, therefore, belong together inseparably: In this history God makes himself known—and therefore the understanding of this history unveils itself also, as soon as we direct
our view to the fact that God acts in it. The Old Testament
teaches us, from its beginning, that we are not without God in
the world, and, at the same time, it opens our eyes to the fact
that our history is not meaningless, because it is included in
God's great plan of history.

CHAPTER

2

The Period of the Judges and Kings

In the first period of its history Israel did not yet live in the
land that would later become its home territory. The Israelites were primarily herdsmen and cattle breeders who lived
in tents and frequently changed their grazing places, even as
the Bedouin do today in the regions of the Near East. But out
of this period came the fundamental traditions of Israel's history and religion. The patriarchal stories tell how God made
himself known from the first to the fathers, how he led them
and blessed them, so that out of them a great nation came into
existence. The tradition of the rescue out of Egypt offers a
testimony about God's great act of salvation, through which
he made himself known to his people as the God of history.
And the account of God's making a covenant with Israel on
Sinai forms the foundation for Israel's special relationship to
God and for the divine law under which Israel was to lead its
life. Thus, in this early period of Israel's history, the foundations for that which came later were already laid. But now
there occurred a process that fundamentally altered the whole
style of life for the Israelites. They exchanged their Bedouin-
like existence in the grassland and desert for the sedentary life
of farmers in a fruitful farmland. How far-reaching this change
was is expressed in the frequent Old Testament description of
this land as "a land flowing with milk and honey." To a person
going today from Europe or America to Palestine it appears

to be a poor land indeed, but compared to the inconceivably impoverished life of the Bedouin it was near to being a paradise.

The change to a sedentary life was not for the Israelites an overnight occurrence. It was a slow and gradual process extending over decades, or perhaps even centuries. Not all the Israelite groups came into the land at the same time; rather, there may have been generations between the settling down of the individual tribes. The tradition has forcibly drawn these processes together. It tells only one small segment out of the events of this period—that occurring under the leadership of Joshua—and it places him in the position of appearing to lead all the tribes. The tradition emphasized one primary point, that of the military encounter with the former inhabitants of the land, the Canaanites. Many battles are told of in which the Israelites defeated the Canaanites and conquered their cities. But these battles certainly will have been only exceptional cases, while there was peaceful coexistence between Israelites and Canaanites most of the time. But it is understandable that the warlike events have remained fixed in memory more strongly than the less dramatic processes of slowly settling down and that they lend themselves to repetition particularly well.

Here again many questions remain for the historian, not all of which can be satisfactorily answered in the long run. Even archaeology cannot solve all the problems; moreover, it gives answers many times that do not harmonize with the Biblical tradition. We should not allow ourselves to be confused by this; rather, we must understand quite clearly that here we have to do with stories that have constantly altered their form in the course of centuries of repetition, just as was the case with the traditions out of the previous period. It would be entirely wrong for us to cling uneasily to the text of these stories and to be unwilling to admit that they have been subject to historical alterations. But it would also be wrong for us to think that these stories have thereby lost their value for us.

They are not documentary accounts in the modern sense, but they do show us how Israel experienced its history under God's guidance. For the thought stands in the foreground here also that God has led his people and that he had shown himself as powerful—as God himself—in his historical acts. And this insight retains its meaning for us even though the stories do not prove to be strictly historical documents in the modern sense.

After the occupation of the land, the individual Israelite tribes continued to lead their own separate lives. We cannot really speak of one "people" Israel in this period; we ought, rather, to speak of a tribal confederacy, a comparatively loose alliance of individual, autonomous tribes. It is important, therefore, to see what the unifying bond was that held the tribes together. Primarily, they felt themselves bound together quite simply in the fact that they had all just changed over from nomadic to sedentary life and that this distinguished them from the former inhabitants, the Canaanites. But this distinction was not merely sociological, that is, it was not marked by a different style of life. What separated the Israelites especially sharply from the Canaanites was their religion. Canaanite religion had many deities. Each god was qualified for a designated area of competence, and one had to pray to him with designated inducements and bring him offerings. One of these deities played a very special role, Baal, the god of fertility. The Canaanites devoted to him an exuberant cult which often took on licentious forms that must have filled the land's newcomers with deep disgust.

The Israelites opposed this cult with their totally different faith in the one God who had until now led and blessed them. They had bound themselves together in a covenant whose most important content was the common worship of this one God. In the twenty-fourth chapter of Joshua we are told how Joshua gathered all the tribes at Shechem and concluded a covenant with them. The Ark of the Covenant became for the tribes a visible sign of the presence of the invisible God. It was the common holy object about which the tribes normally gathered themselves. With this tribal union, which bore the name "Israel," there thus began the second epoch of Israelite history.

When we examine this history more closely, we see that again it was not primarily political processes, but religious, that indelibly stamped the character of this period. On the one hand, the tribal union had come to the place where the traditions of the first epoch were gathered and, so to speak, fused into one great, cohesive portrayal of the origins of Israel. The traditions of the patriarchs, of the rescue out of Egypt, and of the making of the covenant on Sinai were frequently expounded in the gatherings of the tribal union and formed the consciousness of the common history which Israel had experienced under God's guidance. And the divine judgment, which had been proclaimed at the making of the covenant on Sinai, became the basis of their common life. On the other hand, the Israelites had also to come to grips with the Canaanite religion. The Canaanites claimed that their gods were the real lords of the land. They believed that the fertility of the land was due to these gods, and that their whole cult should serve to guarantee the constant renewal of this fertility.

Israel's God, to the contrary, had until now shown himself to be the powerful lord of history who had led his people through all dangers. But was he also the lord of the land and its fertility? Or should one here make some recognition of the Canaanites' claim? This question was not easy for the Israelites to answer. There were strong groups among them who desired to recognize the lordship of the god Baal, or who wanted simply to identify their own God, Yahweh, with the Canaanite god, Baal. But the critical powers in Israel recognized that such mixing or identification was wholly impossible. If Israel's God were really the one, true God, then there could be no area in which he alone could not rule. For this reason, nature was also in the area of his lordship. Thus, the recognition came into being from then on that the God of Israel was the lord not only of history but also of nature. As the one, true God he was the lord and the creator of the world. Israel thus came in this period to a new, deeper knowledge of God, which possesses fundamental significance for us today. Israel learned to understand God as the lord of all aspects of the world and of life. Nothing could be excluded from his lordship. But we must remember once again that the origin of this recognition lay in the fact that Israel had come to know God in his historical activity. Even in the further and deeper understanding of God which was now opened, the thought had never become established in Israel that God would reveal himself in nature. History remained the place in which God encountered men. It was from this that he could be further recognized as the creator and lord of nature.

The tribal alliance was thus in the first instance a religious community. But in specific instances it took on the appearance of a political and, above all, military community as well. This occurred whenever a member of the confederacy was attacked by outsiders. In this case all the other tribes were pledged to offer military aid. But a peculiar characteristic of this commonwealth showed itself at this point: there was no permanent military leader. Who then was to call the tribes together and lead them against the enemy? The Old Testament tradition tells us that in such times of need men would suddenly arise who would take over the leadership. The suddenness, the unexpectedness of their appearance, afforded recognition that the Spirit of God must have come over such men, so that they could call the tribes to arms and lead them in the field. One of the best known of these figures is Gideon, who rescued the Israelites from the marauding Midianites as they frequently invaded the land on their fast camels and laid it waste. The tradition has given these men the name "judges"; in other passages they are called "deliverers," which is the best designation of their function. The term is frequently found in The Book of Judges.

Thus the tribal union was again and again rescued out of

great need through these deliverers. But finally, oppression at the hands of the strong Philistines, the western neighbors of Israel, became so great that the view came to prevail that there must be a permanent military leader. The choice fell on Saul of the tribe of Benjamin. He had already come forward himself as a deliverer taken hold of by the Spirit of God and had been able to repulse an attack by the Ammonites from the East. Now the Israelites installed him as king.

This was a momentous step, for it established in Israel a national organization such as it had never had before, and that meant a break with tradition. The intention of installing a king had evidently surfaced earlier. Thus it is told how the Israelites had offered the office of king to Gideon after his victory over the Midianites; however, he refused them with the significant reason, "I will not rule over you, and my son will not rule over you; the LORD will rule over you" (Judg. 8:23). And this question must also be raised now: How can the installation of a king be harmonized with the exclusive lordship of God over his people? The story of the installation of Saul as king reflects the domestic argument that arose over this question and that was never fully silenced in the succeeding centuries. In one part of the story the demand for a king is described as a falling away from God. Thus the radical answer was given here that the lordship of God and the lordship of a king were mutually exclusive. But there was never more than a small circle in Israel who thought this way.

To us today it might seem natural to adopt the interpretation that God's lordship and human lordship belong to two distinct spheres, so that, rightly understood, they could not overlap each other at all, because human lordship has to do only with the "worldly" sphere in which its commands must be complied with according to human, secular viewpoints. But this thought lay far from that of ancient Israel. It presumes a division of reality into different spheres, a presumption Israel never came to. As Israel never recognized any fundamental distinction between "nature" and "history," so also it never distinguished between "worldly" and "spiritual." Reality always remained for Israel whole and undivided.

Thus the lordship of a king in Israel could be understood only within this one reality, which as a whole is the sphere of God's lordship. And thus it was that the renowned and highly reputable "man of God," Samuel, anointed Saul as king and thereby gave his office divine recognition. A king without such recognition had never been possible for Israel. The king was commissioned and installed by God. This installation could be understood later as an equivalent of adoption, so that the king could be designated as a "son" of God as in other religions of the ancient oriental world (Ps. 2:7). However, he never took on divine qualities as a result, but always remained only God's representative. And he was measured in his kingship as to whether he conformed to the will of God, whether he himself followed in the historical course in which God desired to lead his people, or whether he sought to go his own way.

Here conflicts frequently arose. Political necessities were often stronger for the kings than the question of God's historical plans. And frequently the prophets stood in opposition as watchmen of the tradition, demanding that all policy would have to be subordinated to this question of God's historical plan. Eventually prophets and historical writers often asserted that not only had God chosen a king, but he could also reject him.

The reign of Saul was of only short duration. It was his primary business to dislodge the Philistines from the land; but in the next year they mounted a counterattack, and Saul and his son Jonathan fell in battle against them. But the institution of kingship had meanwhile found recognition among most of the Israelites; the consciousness of being a single people requiring a common head had done its work. Thus David, who had been Saul's armor-bearer, could ascend the throne as his successor.

This began a new, decisive period in Israel's history. David was doubtless the most important figure ever to appear in

Israel's political history. It is certainly not going too far to call him a genius as a statesman. This shows itself in his grasp of domestic affairs. It took a number of years before he was recognized as king over all Israel. At first, only his own tribe of Judah conferred the kingship on him; only later did the other tribes install him as king. But David must have then suspected that tribal rivalries would undermine the inclusiveness of his rule. For this reason, he made himself independent of these rivalries by creating his own residence out of an area not owing allegiance to any one of the tribes. He conquered the city of Jerusalem, which had been previously inhabited by the Jebusites. In this city he possessed a separate, centrally located capital, independent of the tribes. Furthermore, he moved the Ark of the Covenant, the ancient holy object of the tribal confederacy, to Jerusalem. By this means he gave the people of Israel a new religious point of focus. This now unified the civil and the religious centers in one place. The significance that Jerusalem acquired in the following centuries and that it possesses until today for the whole Christian world has its origin in this act of David.

But one ought not to see this as merely an act of political cleverness. It was grounded much more in the whole religious tradition of Israel that there could be no basic separation between religion and politics. And so, for the kingship, everything depended on preserving a close connection with the religious foundation of Israel, which David had done with the bringing of the Ark of the Covenant to Jerusalem. And now came yet a second factor, which gave the figure of David its religious significance for all time. The prophet Nathan announced to him that God himself had made him king over Israel and that his descendants would also be given this kingship. By this prophetic word David was recognized as God's elect, and this religious election gave his kingship a wholly special character. For it tied in now the expectation that God would always be with the family of David. And soon the hope was founded that a king would arise out of the line of David,

who would be wholly after the heart of God and with whom
the time of salvation would begin, a time in which all the trouble of the present would be at an end. It is the expectation of
the Messiah, God's anointed king of the final times, which has
its origin here.

Thus David was virtually the model king in Israel. He made
known his statesmanlike capabilities above all, however, in
foreign affairs. Within a brief period he succeeded in making
the newly resultant state of Israel the dominant power in the
whole area of Syria and Palestine. He defeated and subjugated
the powerful Philistines in the west and the Ammonites, Mo-
abites, and Edomites in the east and south. But he even extended his rule to the north into the area of the Arameans, the
northeastern neighbors, as far as Damascus, and even as far as
the Euphrates. For the circumstances of that time, it was an
enormous area that David was able to unite under his rule.

David's son and successor, Solomon, was a wholly different
sort. He directed his attention much less to political and military matters; in his court he cultivated much more of the arts
and sciences. His great wisdom is told of, and we are informed
that he maintained many international relationships, so that
the cultural life of the great royal courts of the Egyptians and
Babylonians now found entry into Jerusalem also. Out of this
period stem the first great literary works in Israel. These were
mainly the histories of the kings, put forth in several smaller
historical works. These have been transmitted to us in the books
of Samuel, including the story of Saul, David's rise to power,
and the struggles over his succession, which was finally decided
in favor of Solomon. They are splendid stories, among the most
beautiful to be found in the prose tales of the ancient East. At
the same time they are the first genuine historical works that
men anywhere had produced. But the old traditions out of the
origins of Israel's history, passed on orally by the people for centuries, also found now their final literary form. It consists of a
large-scale work that began with the creation of the world and
led up to the Israelites' conquest of Palestine. This work forms

the basic material of the so-called Five Books of Moses. Great sections of the first part of the Old Testament were thus originated in this period of the initial cultural flowering.

But Solomon was seen politically as a weak king. In his lifetime the Israelite rule over neighboring peoples had begun to break up. After his death in the year 926 B.C., the nation broke apart in the middle. It became evident now that the two parts that David had united had separated again. Solomon's son Rehoboam was able to maintain himself as king only over the tribe of Judah, while the northern tribes installed their own king, Jeroboam. There resulted now two small states adjoining each other. The northern, larger part claimed the name Israel, while the southern was designated by its tribal name Judah. With this division the great work of David was effectually smashed.

The succeeding centuries now offer the picture of a politically unimportant history of two small states among the many nations in the region of Syria and Palestine. It was a history of the coexistence and often even the opposition of Israel and Judah. They were soon overshadowed by great political events. In the eighth century before Christ, the Assyrians rose to great power and brought a wide area of the Near East under their rule. In the year 722 B.C. they even made an end to the state of Israel; a greater part of the population was deported and other, foreign population groups were settled in this territory. As a result, this region had virtually no further role in the national and religious history of Israel. Its mixed population was later called Samaritans by the Jews and not reckoned as a portion of the Israelite people.

But even the days of the state of Judah were numbered. In the year 587 B.C. the Babylonians, who had meanwhile come to great power, put it to an end. A part of the population of Judah was also deported. But Judah was saved from the fate of the Northern Kingdom. No foreign population was settled there, so that those remaining in the land were able to keep their traditions unimpaired. And those deported were permitted to live together in Babylonia, so that here also the consciousness of belonging together and the cultivation of the old traditions remained alive, and even a part of the deportees, or their descendants, were later able to return to the land.

Thus the history of the people of Israel was not yet at an end, in spite of the catastrophe. But in retrospect, it yet shows itself as a history of downfall. How could it have come to this? How could this be the outcome of the history of the divine promises given to the people and especially to the house of David? This great historical work has given an answer to this problem, set forth in the books from Joshua through II Kings, the story running from the entry of Israel into the Promised Land to the end of the state of Judah. The answer is that, by the time of the Judges, Israel had fallen away from God, and that affliction at the hands of enemies, frequently encountered, was the consequence of this falling away and was brought about by God himself. But whenever Israel returned to God, then he would send it a deliverer. And a similar interpretation was given in this work to the period of the Kings. The events of the time of the Kings is told in brief, chronological notes that only rarely go beyond the most indispensable matters.

When we read these stories, it strikes us that accompanying the purely historical notes about the reign of the individual kings there normally stands yet a quite different kind of notice. A judgment on the king is expressed there each time, and it normally reads, "He did what was right in the eyes of the LORD," or, "He did what was evil in the sight of the LORD." The kings were thus measured here by religious criteria. The historian can easily claim that by this means many kings who were doubtless capable rulers were nevertheless dismissed with a clearly negative judgment. This judgment is oriented in terms of how well the king in question had maintained the purity of the cult. We have already indicated that the conflict between faith in Israel's God and that in the Canaanite god Baal, a fundamental issue during this whole period, was never resolved. Especially in the Northern Kingdom, the cult of Baal played a major role. Indeed, we even find that there was a large temple to Baal in the capital city of Samaria. Thus the judgment on the kings of the Northern Kingdom in particular is predominantly negative. These judgments had been written down at a time when the period of the Kings was already at an end. For the author of this historical material saw in retrospect that the history of this period also was throughout a story of a falling away from God. For this reason it had to end finally in destruction.

We encounter here again the unity of religion and politics so characteristic of Israel. The political history could not be examined simply for its own sake, because God was active in it. But it can now be seen from this examination of history that the activity of God does not consist merely of his helping his people. To the contrary! The downfall of the people is itself God's activity; it is his judgment on the people who failed to live up to the covenant obligations. The election of Israel is thus in no way a guarantee of security; rather, it signifies the highest responsibility, and it includes the awesome possibility that he holds his people to account. This consciousness was kept alive in Israel especially by certain men who had a decisive voice in the picture of the period of the Kings: the prophets. They had proclaimed the judgment of God time after time, but they had also shown Israel the way into the future after the catastrophe.

3

The Prophets

The nation of Israel experienced its history under the guidance of God. At the beginning of this history stood the promises to the patriarchs, offering them guidance and blessing. And in the rescue out of Egyptian slavery Israel saw God's great, fundamental act of salvation. In spite of this, the story did not move along smoothly. After the great time of David's acquisition of power and the cultural development under Solomon, Israel's political situation went more and more downhill. The nation crumbled away into two independent states; the larger Northern Kingdom was destroyed by the Assyrians in 722 B.C., the smaller Southern Kingdom fell victim to the acquisitive violence of the Babylonians in 587 B.C. That spelled the end of independent political history for Israel's people for the next two and one half millenniums. Had thus the promises on which Israel relied proved false? Or was Israel's God, known as the one, true God and the lord and creator of the world, not yet powerful enough to prevent the downfall of his people? In view of the catastrophe, Israel had to pose these questions. But they were by no means new. For centuries men had come forward to caution and warn Israel against living in false security. These were the prophets, those figures who had so decisive a voice in the history and the religion of Israel.

We have already encountered the prophets in the history of Israel. The tradition had already given Abraham and Moses this title and had expressed thereby the special relation to God in which these men stood. However, we meet the prophets primarily in the period of the Kings.

What, really, is a prophet? Two main characteristics indicate the nature of a prophet. One is his awareness of God, which often makes a difference in visible appearance. Sometimes it is recounted that prophets experience a religious trance rising to the pitch of ecstasy. Although this occurs in many religions, it is not such religious awareness that earns the name of prophecy. A second essential element must be added, that of speaking by the commission of God. That is the real mark of a prophet—that he comes forward with the claim that he speaks in the name and commission of God. It is not easy for us today to understand and evaluate this claim. We no longer have prophets of this sort, and when men come forward today with such a claim, we have good reason to meet them with extreme caution, if not with outright suspicion. Prophecy has had its time. But there can be no doubt that the prophets, in their time, could point to quite real encounters with God, and that their contemporaries also recognized this claim. That there were prophets is an indispensable part of Israel's history.

The prophets were certainly often quite peculiar figures who were frequently regarded with scorn and not taken seriously. It would, nevertheless, be quite wrong to regard them as outside the normal course of things. Very often their words spoke to the crucial issues. Such was the case with the first important prophetic figure at the beginning of the period of the Kings. This was the prophet Nathan, who lived during David's time at the royal court in Jerusalem, and who delivered to King David the divine promise that God had chosen him and his descendants and would bless them, as is told in II Samuel, ch. 7. He thereby laid a decisive foundation for the significance that David's dynasty was to have in the following centuries; it found unlimited acknowledgment in Judah, and God's promise, given through Nathan, stood again and again at the center. At the same time, his words contained the germ of the ex-

pectation of a future king from the line of David, the Messiah,
an expectation that later was to acquire such great significance.
Thus, the prophetic word had here a completely positive function.

Yet, we find that in the following centuries the prophets
were often in an extremely critical position with regard to
their people. The first great confrontation is told us out of the
middle of the ninth century before Christ. It was the time during which King Ahab ruled in Samaria, the capital city of the
Northern Kingdom. As his predecessors had already done, he
allowed Canaanite culture to play a decisive role in his kingdom and had given the Canaanite cult of Baal full freedom.
This politics of religion was so far supported that Ahab mar-
ried a king's daughter from the Phoenician coastal city of Tyre,
where Baal was worshiped as well. Queen Jezebel now urged
the expansion of the Baal cult by all means available; it even
went so far as the persecution of the true followers of Israel's
God, the prophets in particular. Thus it was all too understandable that the people devoted themselves to the cult of
Baal.

In the midst of this situation appeared the prophet Elijah,
who had escaped Queen Jezebel's pursuit. He relentlessly put
the decision before the people, asking: "How long will you
go limping with two different opinions? If the LORD is God,
follow him; but if Baal, then follow him." In I Kings, ch. 18,
we are told of the dramatic confrontation between Elijah and
the representatives of the Baal religion, who were also regarded
as prophets. It was a dispute involving life and death, not only
in that the life of Elijah hung by it, but in that it involved the
life of the people. Israel had become a people through the
unifying bond of belief in the one God; it had experienced
its whole history as the guidance of this God, and the sentence
"I am the LORD your God, . . . you shall have no other gods
before me" stood at the head of the commandments that
formed the foundation for the life of the people. If this foundation were given up, it would mean the end of the people of

Israel! The decision that Elijah put before the people was not a choice between two equivalent possibilities; it was a decision concerning the existence or the nonexistence of the people.

It was due to Elijah that the people of Israel was called back to itself. At the same time, it decided once again for the one, true God and thereby escaped the fate of sinking into the world of Canaanite religion of abandoning itself. This first great confrontation shows what an important role the prophets played in the history of Israel. They did not, as some have sometimes suggested, bring a new religion. To the contrary, they protected the tradition out of which Israel's life had sprung. They sought time and again to prevent Israel from becoming untrue to itself and its history.

The full depth of this danger is recognizable for us in retrospect. But at the same time it becomes clear that our own history was at stake. Had Israel not found the way back to the God of its fathers and to its history, had it dissolved into its religious environment, then the story of Jesus and the Christian church could not have taken the course it did. It is idle to inquire what would have happened in such a case. And it is of much greater import for us that the story turned out as it did —that Israel again became conscious of its inescapable religious involvement and remained conscious of it. For our history as Christians hangs on this history of Israel, and we have God none other than through this history.

But the question that Elijah forced the Israelites to face persists. For us as well, there can be no optional choice between different religious possibilities. For us as well, there persists an inseparable connection between our Christian faith and our history, rooted deeply in Israel's history. We cannot separate the two from each other and we must remain conscious of this connection. Today's much-blamed and much-abused "Christian West" is a reality whose significance we can scarcely value highly enough. Quite certainly, it matters little if it be defended as a cultural value in itself. But just as certainly, it establishes the ground in which we are rooted, together with all that we are. New strength can develop for it and for us only out of a conscious participation in the living stream of our Christian history.

The dangers of which the prophets warned lay, however, not only in the religious area. A few hundred years after Elijah quite different problems meet us in the prophet Amos. His proclamation directs itself primarily against a newly existent group of people, the wealthy. Therein is reflected a process of social change that took place in the first centuries of the time of the Kings. At the beginning of Israel's history the property holdings of all Israelites were approximately the same. They were cattle growers, and later, farmers and wine-growers, and each had what he needed for himself and his family. The economy expanded, and, notably among the urban population, social distinctions became more and more marked. A class of wealthy merchants sprang up who openly and ruthlessly exploited the poor, and as a result often sold them into slavery for indebtedness.

Amos appeared with an accusation of unheard-of sharpness against this activity. Such doings, he saw, shook the foundations of the life of Israel, for this was more than a social question. Israel lived in the covenant established by God, meaning that every person belonging to the people, as a member of this covenant, had the same rights. For this reason it represented a deep disturbance in Israel's relationship to God for one group within the people to live at the expense of the others, for anyone unscrupulously to set himself up as the lord of the others and even, as Amos so often reproached them, to use unfair means to accomplish it.

Here is shown the deepest root of the demand for equal rights for all. That which today is regarded in the civilized world as an irrevocable claim—however little it may be realized in particular cases—has its origin in this basic awareness of the Israelite religion that through God's covenant with his people each person has equal rights before God and thereby before men as well. At the same time, this shows that this religion cannot be a separate sphere with little or no connection with everyday life. The prophets always fought such a separation most sharply. Life's actuality is an indissoluble unity. There is no such thing as a religious sphere over against a profane sphere. And this whole indissoluble reality always has to do with God. Amos saw the shame of his people very clearly. He held that the time had already come, that Israel had destroyed the basis of its relationship to God himself. Thus his words were not, in the first instance, a call to turn back from the false way, but a proclamation of the imminent judgment of God on his people. But this judgment was not a denial of the election of the people, for this formed the basis of his thought and faith. Amos announced rather that it was the direct consequence of that election:

> You only have I known
> of all the families of the earth;
> therefore I will punish you
> for all your iniquities.
>   (Amos 3:2.)

That was for his contemporaries a quite unexpected, astonishing, and shocking consequence: "Therefore I will punish you for all your iniquities." What kind of "therefore" is that? One would have expected a positive outcome from God's elective act, a gracious, healing, comforting outcome such as had always been a part of the religious tradition until now. Instead, there was this harsh dissonance, this glaring paradox: Because God had chosen Israel, therefore he would punish it for its iniquities! Ought it not read: "Therefore he would forgive its iniquities"? Amos' hearers would certainly have expected so—if iniquities really had to be spoken of at all.

But here lay the decisive misunderstanding: Israel felt as if election were a guarantee for an unalterably gracious relationship with God. Election, however, means responsibility, and, where this responsibility is disregarded, God will hold Israel to account for its election.

Amos understood the iniquities of Israel in a very concrete
sense. He had in mind primarily that area of life which we
would call "social." But Amos was no social reformer; rather,
he required of the Israelites what had already formed the basis of their life together, that within the covenant that God had
concluded with the people of Israel each person should have
his right undiminished, even if he were too weak to grasp it for
himself. They were thus not primarily "religious" offenses with
which Amos reproached the Israelites. Their worship might
be ever so exact and "correct," but Amos denied that that was
sufficient to do justice to the responsibility involved in
election. He had come to realize that the cult, the worship of
God, was widely understood as a guarantee that granted to
the other areas of life complete freedom and lack of restraint.
And he proclaimed that God renounced such divine worship
and wanted no part of it. Jeremiah had later in a similar situation reproached his contemporaries: they had made the
Temple a den of robbers. So, as robbers between raids kept
themselves in safety in their hiding places, so the Israelites
did likewise when they intended to put in order their relationship to God in worship while trampling on it when outside.
And these insights have maintained their undiminished reality
until today. Jesus stood wholly in the line of the Old Testament prophets when he put love of neighbor next to love of
God as the first commandment; and the same thing holds today that was true in the time of Amos: worship and all the
other elements of the religious life are worthless if they do not
accord with the right relationship to the neighbor.

Amos proclaimed to his people God's judgment. He spoke
particularly to the inhabitants of the Northern Kingdom, appearing at their great shrine in Bethel. And just a few decades
later his proclamation was fulfilled: the Northern Kingdom fell
victim to the attack of the Assyrians. The prophets were not
mere preachers appealing to the conscience of the people.
They proclaimed God's imminent historical action. And it is
not a matter of indifference to us that what they proclaimed

was fulfilled. The truth of their proclamation is shown last but
not least in a historical fulfillment. For if God really acts in history, and if the prophets have really spoken on behalf of God,
then there must certainly be a connection between the two.
The history of Israel shows us how close this connection was,
with what uncanny consistency the things happened which
the prophets announced. It shows us yet something else: that
God acts toward Israel, that God directs its history, means for
Israel itself something completely other than passivity, a mere
allowing to happen whatever God does. Israel is thereby involved in the highest measure. Its history is denoted by the
tension between God's plan, which is directed toward salvation, and Israel's behavior, which frequently stands opposed
to this plan. And the fate of Israel shows that God's action can
also result in judgment on his elect people. That does not
mean the end of election, but it shows unequivocally that
election is no guarantee of security, making Israel's own acts
superfluous and meaningless. And, conversely, it is clear that
God's action is not, without further ado, to be taken to mean
the well-being of the chosen people. Obviously, God can act
against his people as well.

The Christian church sees itself in succession to Israel in this
tension-filled interaction of election and responsibility. It can
be confident in its historically rooted election and can rest
assured that God will carry to its goal his plan for it and for
the world. But there is not a moment of freedom from responsibility for the Christian church's behavior, not only for its actions as a corporate body, but for the actions of its members
as well. For the church's responsibility must be confirmed in
the responsible lives of those who belong to it. For our nation
—which, according to tradition, is on the whole Christian—
that means, however, nothing more or less than that the behavior of this entire nation, like that of other Christian nations,
will inevitably be seen as an expression of this responsibility
of the church. If the church wants to be found again only in
the tiny circle of its own faithful, that will itself be a retreat

from its historical responsibility. But this responsibility remains to be endured and it demands from each one who acknowledges it all his powers of compliance.

At about the same time that Amos appeared in the Northern Kingdom, another great prophet worked in Jerusalem, one whose name has resounded most forcefully: Isaiah. His proclamation extended over many decades and covered many things. In him also one finds vehement attacks against the wealthy, against speculators in houses and land who trampled on the fundamental Israelite law by which each one held an allotted piece of land:

> Woe to those who join house to house,
>   who add field to field,
> until there is no more room,
>   and you are made to dwell alone
>   in the midst of the land.
>
> (Isa. 5:8.)

But it was primarily the political realm into which he so frequently intervened with his prophetic word. This shows again, and especially impressively, how much the prophets with their proclamation were rooted in the old traditions of Israel. In an hour of greatest threat Isaiah challenged King Ahaz to faith:

> If you will not believe,
>   surely you shall not be established.
>
> (Isa. 7:9.)

What does it signify that Isaiah should speak of faith in such a situation? Two motives are brought close together here. One is the knowledge that God has previously directed the history of his people. The other is the confidence that he will direct it in the future as well. Faith is not a foolhardy and uncertain undertaking; it has its firm roots in the historical action of God in the past. Isaiah could have spoken about the ancient traditions and historical experiences prior to the king

at length here; he could have reminded him of the divine promises, especially of the promises given to David and his line,
to which Ahaz belonged. But he had no need of doing so, for
Ahaz knew all that. He knew very well what was intended;
he knew that he should base his confidence on the fact that
God, as in past times even so now, held the events of history
in his hand. But he did not find the courage for this confidence.
He preferred, rather, to put his hopes on some strong allies,
even though he had to realize that it would cost him his political independence. And for this reason he submitted himself to the mighty Assyrian king and begged him for help
against the aggressors. That meant, however, that Ahaz really
gave himself up. "If you will not believe, surely you shall not
be established," said Isaiah. "Be established" meant, however,
not merely "survive"; it did not mean only that Jerusalem
would remain safe from destruction. It meant "to have permanence," which reminds one quite clearly of the promise
that had been given to David through Nathan: that his kingdom should have permanence. But it was to be a kingdom
from the hand of God, and now Ahaz had made it into a kingdom from the hand of the Assyrian king. The price that Ahaz
paid was too high: he had surrendered himself.

Again, in this confrontation between King Ahaz and the
prophet Isaiah the question arises as to whether religion is
only one sphere among others, and indeed, here in particular,
whether religion and politics are two spheres having nothing
to do with each other. King Ahaz wanted to separate them;
he had no wish to allow Isaiah to lecture him about his political concepts. Isaiah vehemently denied the propriety of
this separation: the only proper political attitude for him was
one which unreservedly acknowledged the hand of God. But
is that not an unrealistic fanaticism? Is it not right to call Isaiah's political claims utopian? Do these presuppositions allow
any politics at all? Most certainly, but not so that one could
all at once rely on God's intervention, if one's politics previously had been wholly without these presuppositions. For

this reason it would be misleading for us simply to transfer the claims of Isaiah to the present time and seek to draw firm political conclusions for our political action from them, as is not infrequently attempted today.

We must first of all pose Isaiah's basic question: whether we shape our politics right from the start under the presupposition that God is at work in historical events. And we can learn from the history of Israel that this must mean primarily that the preceding history is to be understood as God's action. We must thereupon ask what might be learned from history on the basis of this presupposition. And only then can consequences be yielded for future action. We are infinitely far from all that. But we shall have to put this question to ourselves seriously if we do not want to gamble away irreparably the heritage of our Christian people and the Christian West, so much blamed and abused today.

To acknowledge the action of God in history does not mean only that God will protect his people. Amos had proclaimed the judgment of God on the Northern Kingdom of Israel. And in Isaiah's proclamation the threatening shadow of this history stood out over the Southern Kingdom of Judah also in an even more threatening manner. There yet remained for the Southern Kingdom a period in which it could pretend to a modest existence as an Assyrian vassal state. But even that led to its end. The prophet Jeremiah accompanied the last phase of Judah's history with his words. For him it was easy to see that God would lead his people into judgment. He no longer proclaimed salvation from this threat, but demanded that the inhabitants of Judah and Jerusalem submit themselves to the yoke of the king of Babylonia. It is all too clear that Jeremiah with this pushed them all the way to refusal. They clung to the ancient promises that God would rescue his people, and they hoped for a miracle yet this one time. But Jeremiah announced that the time of God's mercy was now at an end, that Israel must now pass through judgment.

The Old Testament tells us that there were other prophets

as well in the time of Jeremiah, who proclaimed quite the opposite. They boasted of the ancient promises and proclaimed that the danger to the nation would soon be at an end, that it could soon live in peace again. Jeremiah charged that these prophets were "saying, 'Peace, peace,' when there is no peace." They preached what everyone wanted to hear. They pacified the people and deceived them about the true situation. But he is no true prophet who says what the people expect to hear, but only he who speaks the truth to them. And the truth is often bitter and hard. But it alone makes free. Jeremiah saw the actual situation of his people before God. He knew that God had destined it to pass through the dark depths of judgment, and he challenged the nation to consent to this. He wanted to inspire his people's courage to go through this hard time with confidence in God. It is easy to believe, in good times, that God directs history. But, if one goes through the "valley of the shadow of death" of which the psalmist speaks, then will be displayed how deeply this faith is grounded and whether it really sustains.

What Jeremiah had announced came true. Jerusalem was overcome by the Babylonians and a portion of the inhabitants were deported to Babylonia. Did that mean the end? Were the promises now of no more worth, and were all the earlier experiences of God's guidance proven lies by hard reality? But that could not and must not be! The mood among those deported wavered between total resignation and exaggerated expectation. Indeed, these two extremes were apparently the only possibilities: either God had abandoned his people, in which case all was over, or he stood by it yet, in which case this would be only a short interval, brought to a quick end through a mighty intervention of God. And so it was the bearers of Israel's traditions of faith, the prophetic group, who proclaimed that God would soon turn the fate of his people toward the good.

Preserved in the twenty-ninth chapter of Jeremiah is a letter that Jeremiah had written to the deportees. It shows that

Jeremiah did not acknowledge these alternatives. God has not abandoned his people; he stands by them. But he has, himself, brought on this catastrophe; it is his judgment on Israel. The reckoning does not add up if Israel thinks that its welfare is the measure of God's action. For in this reckoning a decisive factor is missing: Israel's own responsibility for the history it was wrecked on. The tradition of faith makes a caricature of itself if it tries to make God the guarantee of the welfare of the people without looking back at how this people had conducted itself. In this distortion the tradition can no longer be the ground on which the people in the present time draw their strength. For then there can be only resignation or rebellion over against their present time.

Jeremiah apparently stands against the tradition. But he has historical reality on his side—and thereby the tradition as well! For tradition is never something closed; it can never be placed against historical reality as a self-contained quantity, but it extends into it, is inseparably intertwined with it, and is constantly developed through it. Jeremiah freely puts into practice the theme of the tradition that God acts in every occurrence. For this reason, he cannot exclude even this dark present; he cannot add that God acts only when the course of his people seems bright and cheerful.

The relationship to history is decided in the present. It establishes for us our historical duties. We are called upon to do now what is required. We must not allow ourselves to muddy our view, lest we grieve after things past or dream of a better future. Past and future are included in God's action; but he has shown us our place in the present.

Jeremiah's instructions to the deportees were extremely sensible: to build houses, to plant gardens, to contract marriages, to beget children—thus to do all that has been given mankind to do. This certainly does not mean so to act as if nothing had happened. Jeremiah had often said unequivocally that the present situation was God's judgment on Israel; and he frequently proclaimed that there was to be a future and a hope for Israel. Both belong to the understanding of the present. But this knowledge about past and future makes it necessary to live in the present now and to make a beginning with the duties given to us here and now.

This letter of Jeremiah has gained for us again a startling reality. The consciousness that the present situation cannot be final is in vogue among many of us, above all among those who have been wholly separated by the present concrete walls and barbed wire from others with whom they are inseparably bound by a common history. Resignation and desperate hope for an early change lie for them all too near. But we know also that this letter of Jeremiah is frequently read by them and that many seek to understand the darkened present as their God-appointed place in history and to fulfill the duties given them, in sorrow, anguish, and private, cautious hope.

But also for us others, who live in direct view of the walls, or at least hear of them daily, the provisionality of our present situation is again rudely thrust into our consciousness. If we do not close our eyes to it, our hands can be paralyzed and we can be led into the temptation to wait just a little longer until the times have again returned to "normal." So we are no less in need of Jeremiah's admonition to take seriously our historical place in the present and to fulfill our duties in it.

Above all, however, we must not seek to shield ourselves from all this and act as if nothing had happened. That would be the worst misunderstanding of our historical situation, and it could happen this way to us, that we could become before God as bad figs which can only be cast away (Jer., ch. 24). We can take the present seriously only when we see it in its connection with the past—and with the future. For over it, dark though it be, stand the words from Jeremiah's letter: "For I know the plans I have for you, says the LORD, plans for welfare and not for evil, to give you a future and a hope." Future history is God's history, as was the past.

CHAPTER

4

The Psalms

The Psalms have an especially firm place among the Old Testament books in Christian worship and in the personal religious life of many Christians. Numerous passages from the Psalms are so well known and familiar to us that we hardly ever stop to think that they come from the Old Testament and not from the New. Moreover, the Psalms are printed as an appendix in the most-used editions of the New Testament, a fact that also expresses an awareness of its close connection. We shall now direct our attention to the inner relationship of the Psalms with the rest of the Old Testament so that we may learn to understand the Psalms also as a testimony to the history of the people of Israel, which history was experienced as God's action.

The collection of one hundred and fifty psalms passed on to us in the Old Testament is recognizable as the songbook of Israel. Just as in our hymnals songs from the Reformation, and even translations and rewritings of yet older songs, are mixed in with others from the succeeding centuries down to our own time, and just as these songs have been composed and sung for quite various reasons, so also the psalms encompass a wide period of time and the most varied occasions. And, just as in our hymnals, psalms which are an expression of the faith of the congregation gathered in worship stand next to those which speak of a wholly personal piety.

We know unfortunately little about how the details of worship were conducted in Old Testament times. But the psalms show us clearly that at many points in the worship service the congregation, perhaps in alternation with a choir, expressed their adoration and praise as well as their laments and petitions. Worship was certainly more outwardly exciting than it is with us today. We often hear that the participants entered the Temple in festive procession. Thus it is to be taken quite literally when it says in Psalm 100,

> Enter his gates with thanksgiving,
>   and his courts with praise!

or in Psalm 118,

> Open to me the gates of righteousness,
>   that I may enter through them
>   and give thanks to the LORD.

Psalm 24, which we know so well from Advent, stems also from such a festival procession:

> Lift up your heads, O gates!
>   and be lifted up, O ancient doors!
>   that the King of glory may come in.

Here it is not only the participants in the service who enter the Temple but God himself as well. The entry of the Ark of the Covenant is certainly in mind here, it being the visible sign of the presence of the invisible God. The psalm thus reflects a festive procession with the Ark of the Covenant, in which God himself enters the Temple. These examples serve to show how the Psalms give us many particulars about the outward performance of the worship service.

But we must now pursue the primary question raised by the Psalms: how they gave expression to the faith of Israel. We have already brought out how Israel saw its whole existence as grounded in the great historical act of God's salvation. So also in the Psalms these fundamental events are spoken of. Many psalms repeat the whole story from the exodus out of Egypt to the entry into the Promised Land. They speak of how God "with a strong hand and an outstretched arm" rescued his people from slavery, or how "the horse and his rider he has thrown into the sea" in order to save his people. They praise the wonders that God did in the wilderness when he gave his people manna and quails and caused water to gush from the rock. And they portray the acts through which God allowed his people finally to enter into the Promised Land.

But the range covered is yet wider: The Psalms praise God as the creator of the world. We have already spoken of how in Israel the experience of God's historical actions stood at the beginning and how then later the awareness grew that this God of history was also the lord and creator of the world. This can be clearly recognized in the Psalms as well. As an example let us choose Psalm 136. It begins with a sentence frequently found in the Psalms:

> O give thanks to the LORD, for he is good,
> for his steadfast love endures for ever.

This exclamation, "for his steadfast love endures for ever," is repeated after each verse throughout the psalm; obviously, we have here an antiphony between choir and congregation. In this antiphony God is at first praised as the creator:

> to him who by understanding made the heavens,
> . . . .
> to him who spread out the earth upon the waters,
> . . . .
> to him who made the great lights,
> . . . .
> the sun to rule over the day,
> . . . .
> the moon and stars to rule over the night.

But suddenly the psalm moves from creation to history:

> to him who smote the first-born of Egypt,
> . . . .
> and brought Israel out from among them,
> . . . .
> with a strong hand and an outstretched arm.

Then follows the portrayal of God's act of salvation in history. Here, the creation is almost a mere facade; it is a preparation for that within which God will reveal himself to his people and show himself as the lord of all history.

In this psalm, God's creative action is spoken of in the same manner as we find in the creation story in Genesis; it is put in clear, simple sentences: he created, he established, he made. But we find in the Psalms wholly different expressions as well, which strike us as being very strange. It is said that God had fought with the sea, that he broke the heads of the dragon, and had defeated the sea monster Rahab. Peculiar scenes, which scarcely accord with what the Old Testament otherwise says about God! They are remnants of the religious tradition of other nations of the ancient East. Especially in Babylonia there was an ancient myth that told how in the beginning the primeval sea had revolted against the gods, creating heaven and earth out of the corpse of the monster. Obviously, Israel also knew these old stories. But it testifies to the great religious strength of this people that it could take up such traditions—and many others could be mentioned—and fuse them into its own understanding of God. We are encountering here a process whose significance we can scarcely overestimate: The little nation of Israel, which entered the world of the great religions of the Near East as a novice, had, with its faith in the one, true God, unflinchingly made its way against the primitive traditions of its environment. It took up many various themes from the other religions, but it fused them all and made them useful to its avowal that only this one God existed and that he alone was the lord. Here again it becomes clear how much the history of Israel's religion is our history. We stand quite obviously on this ground which Israel had created in its encounter with the other religions.

The claim of Israel over against the other religions is given expression in the Psalms primarily where God is praised as a king. "The LORD reigns." So begins a series of psalms. Even

the other peoples have gods who are given the royal title. But
Israel opposes them with this cry: "The LORD reigns!" It is at
the same time a renunciation of all other claims:

> He is to be feared above all gods.
> For all the gods of the peoples are idols;
> but the LORD made the heavens.

So Psalm 96 puts it. The gods of the peoples are nothing—
this insight developed in Israel over the course of the centuries.
In the beginning, the Israelites also believed that there were
other gods who were worshiped by the other peoples; but more
and more the awareness developed that the one, true God,
who had revealed himself above all to the people Israel, was
not only the greatest and most powerful among the gods, but
that he alone was really God, and that the gods of the other
peoples were nothing. In speaking of God as the king of the
gods, the old conception still shines through; but the newly
won awareness, that there was only one God, now rules the
whole.

When God is praised as king, it is at the same time an expression about his relationship to the world. As king, God is
not enthroned inaccessibly in the remoteness of heaven, but
he is the king of the nations, and by this the nations are also
included in his historical action. God directs not only the history of Israel but the fate of all peoples. The prophets also
frequently spoke of how the whole of history was God's action; they included in this view the great actors in the world's
history—the Egyptians, the Assyrians, the Babylonians, the
Persians. And the Psalms conceive this in the form of a confession:

> God reigns over the nations;

and

> He will judge the world with righteousness,
> and the peoples with his truth.

In order fully to understand the audacity of this thought, we must remind ourselves once again of the political situation in the Near East. The two great power blocs, Egypt and Mesopotamia, ruled over everything. Palestine was a plaything of their interests and confrontations. Only in a small breathing space was it possible for David to exist and to win his own area of rule in the space between the two power blocs. But a little later, after the death of Solomon, this structure crumbled away, and from then on the nation of Israel was occupied with world politics only passively, while, for the most part enduring whatever the great powers did to it. Nevertheless, we find this audacious statement about the world rule of Israel's God. We recognize here the basis of the Christian understanding of the world and of history, which Israel had been able to preserve even through the centuries of deepest political impotence.

But in the Psalms, history is spoken of not solely in tones of unflinching confidence. As in the prophetic proclamation of judgment and in the relentless presentation of Israel's downfall in the books of Kings, so also in the Psalms we encounter testimonies of deep insight into the sin of Israel and its inseparable involvement with the course of history. Psalm 106 offers an especially expressive example. It also tells the story of Israel's history, as we know it from other psalms. It speaks not only of what God has done, but each time it places over against it the things Israel had done. Thus it says of the earliest beginning of salvation history:

> Our fathers, when they were in Egypt,
>   did not consider thy wonderful works;
> they did not remember the abundance of thy
>   steadfast love,
>   but rebelled. . . .

And then the whole story is unfolded as a history of rebellion and backsliding from God and of divine sentence and judgment. It carries on until the captivity and dispersion of the people.

In many psalms we hear the lament of those who remained behind in the ruins of Jerusalem after the collapse of the Kingdom of Judah or who had been led into captivity. One particular collection of such lamentations out of Jerusalem is preserved for us, the so-called Lamentations of Jeremiah. And out of the captivity come psalms such as Psalm 137, which begins:

> By the waters of Babylon,
>   there we sat down and wept,
>   when we remembered Zion.

Everywhere there sounds more or less clearly the knowledge that Israel itself had incurred this its fate. But in most psalms the lament is not left as the last word. Frequently a confident plea for help is lifted up; ever more strongly the gaze is directed to the future, to the yet-impending action of God. History is by no means at an end. God has sentenced his people, but he has not crushed it. His faithfulness persists throughout history.

The faithfulness of God—that is the major theme which sounds throughout a great part of the Psalms. And often, where in our Bibles the goodness or the grace of God is spoken of, "faithfulness" would be a better translation. This expresses the belief that this attitude of God, so little deserved by Israel, is yet not unforeseen and unexpected, but has its deep roots in all that God had earlier done for his people. When God does not fully reject Israel, then he remains true to himself right to the final end. That is really the specific idea that gives this history its inner cohesion.

This knowledge that the faithfulness of God is the ground of all things finds its clearest expression in the statement already cited:

> O give thanks to the LORD, for he is good,
>   for his steadfast love endures for ever!

For our ears this word perhaps no longer has the full, strong ring it possessed for the Israelites, especially since we employ it as a table grace. But we shall endeavor to regain this strong ring. "Praise the Lord," we could better translate the beginning of it, for it does not refer to a feeling of thankfulness, but the public praise of the congregation. Indeed, the word can even mean "acknowledge." It is a strong expression of that which now follows, which the whole congregation and each individual in it should acknowledge: "For he is good." That God is good, as is said here, means that he is the source of all human happiness and welfare. That anything at all can be good has its basis solely in the fact that God is good. And then the conclusion, "For his steadfast love endures forever." God's faithfulness exists from the beginning of the world and it continues until the end of the world. It is the ground and measure of all things. Thus this sentence brings together everything that can be said in looking back at the past and in looking forward to the future: the acknowledgment that God is good and does good, and the confidence that his faithfulness exists and that therefore in all the future he will be and do good. This is what the Old Testament means by faith—firm reliance on God's historical action in the past and firm confidence in his future activity.

This keynote of confidence in the faithfulness of God dominates a great part of the Psalms; and it is precisely these psalms which have a firm place in the Christian tradition as well. We need think only of Psalm 90, which has resounded and is still resounding unnumbered times at the important stations of human life:

Lord, thou hast been our dwelling place
    in all generations.
Before the mountains were brought forth,
    or ever thou hadst formed the earth and the world,
    from everlasting to everlasting thou art God.

Here, confidence in the unalterable faithfulness of God constitutes the ground on which all the rest stands, and it is deeply anchored in the past, back to the time of creation or even before the beginning of the world. God stands with his faithfulness at the beginning, before all other occurrences. But this psalm knows also that the disorders of life do not come by chance:

> For we are consumed by thy anger;
> by thy wrath we are overwhelmed.
> Thou hast set our iniquities before thee,
> our secret sins in the light of thy countenance.

Here is shown that this psalm is not merely an elegy about the transitoriness of human life, but that it speaks out of a very concrete, deep experience of distress. The congregation that is praying here has experienced what it means when God's wrath comes upon it. Nevertheless, there also stands at the conclusion the confident plea:

> Return, O LORD! How long?
> Have pity on thy servants!
> Satisfy us in the morning with thy steadfast love,
> that we may rejoice and be glad all our days.

And this is no plea in the midst of uncertainty, but it has its basis in the experience of God's faithfulness and in the knowledge that every happening lies in his hand. Therefore it says finally:

> Let thy work be manifest to thy servants,
> and thy glorious power to their children.

It is a plea that God will open the eyes of his own that they might acknowledge his works, which happen everywhere, and that thereby his glory may be seen to be real. It is good when we bear in mind the larger context in which just one such psalm stands and when we not only give ourselves emotionally to the beautiful, often heard, words, but make ourselves conscious that here, in a quite straightforward manner, the historical experience of centuries is spoken of, the experience on which our Christian faith as well rests.

In this psalm the congregation is speaking. But in many others we encounter the "I" of an individual worshiper. A large group of these psalms speak out of a deep distress:

Out of the depths I cry to thee, O LORD!
Lord, hear my voice!

They are the most diverse forms of distress and danger that we encounter in these psalms: sickness in various forms, often approaching death; persecution, accusation, and slander, which bring the worshiper into grievous temptation and to loneliness and isolation, while even his family and closest friends become his enemies; and often the knowledge of one's own sins, which the worshiper must understand as causing all the deserved consequences that happened to him; and finally, as the last and deepest form of distress and temptation, the thought of being forsaken by God: "My God, my God, why hast thou forsaken me?" So begins Psalm 22, which even Jesus had prayed in the hour of his death, according to the tradition of the Gospels.

If we seek to discover from these psalms a precise picture of the situation in which the worshiper stands, we certainly shall not succeed very often. The statements about sickness, persecution, sin, and forsakenness cross over one another and become entangled. The reason for this is that many of these psalms are not the private prayers of an individual Israelite, but were frequently used prayers—just as we also many a time, when we seek for words in a difficult situation in order to give voice to our distress in prayer, have recourse to verses of a hymn or of a psalm. Thus these psalms have often been used as prayers, and frequently they have served as an expression of some other problem. The Psalms are thus not only Israel's hymnal for use in worship services, they are also a prayer book out of which the individual has often drawn support!

But also in these psalms which express the deepest distress and loneliness, confidence in the faithfulness of God always has the last word:

Nevertheless I am continually with thee;
thou dost hold my right hand.
Thou dost guide me with thy counsel,
and afterward thou wilt receive me to glory.

So reads, for example, Psalm 73. These expressions of confidence are, however, wholly rooted in what we have come to know as the experience of Israel's people in its history and what was constantly present to every Israelite. For the piety of the individual and the confession of the congregation are not unrelated to each other. On what ground ought the individual stand, if he looks only to his own situation and his own experiences? Only in the larger context of his people's history and God's history generally does his life derive its meaning. Indeed, everyone has to bear his own destiny. But it would have been quite unthinkable for an Israelite to consider his own situation apart; he knew that it was inseparably involved with the situation of his people. This recognition has gone far from us; we regard it as an achievement of modern thought that each is responsible only to himself, and his destiny is his own private affair. But in this we submit to a great deception. Precisely the political situation we are in today places inescapably before our eyes once more how closely the individual's destiny is bound together with that of the nation and even of humanity.

Thus, these expressions of confidence are based not solely on that which the individual has experienced. But this sort of thing is often spoken of in the Psalms. There are songs of thanksgiving which tell of direct rescue out of distress and thank God for it. But frequently such thanksgiving psalms then turn their attention to what God has already done earlier, what he always does, and what he will further do. We may select, as just one sample, the well-known and familiar Psalm 103:

> Bless the LORD, O my soul;
>> and all that is within me, bless his holy name!
> Bless the LORD, O my soul,
>> and forget not all his benefits.

This psalm begins as an expression of a person who has experienced God's grace and help, but then its words move away from concern for the individual's own fate:

> The LORD is merciful and gracious,
> slow to anger and abounding in steadfast love.

This statement does not stem solely from the individual's experience, but it brings together the experiences of many:

> He does not deal with us according to our sins,
> nor requite us according to our iniquities.

And now follow statements that sound almost like fixed rules according to which God acts. The experience of generations and of centuries has enabled God's faithfulness to appear in so many forms that one can now speak comprehensively of it:

> For as the heavens are high above the earth,
> so great is his steadfast love toward those who fear him;
> as far as the east is from the west,
> so far does he remove our transgressions from us.
> As a father pities his children,
> so the LORD pities those who fear him.

Thus the historical experiences of Israel are reflected in the Psalms in various ways. The personal religion that finds its expression here is rooted in God's action in the past; but it directs itself ever and again to the yet imminent future deeds of God.

5

Expectation and Hope

We have to this point pursued the history of the people of Israel as it has been preserved in the Old Testament. We have seen how, along with the history of Israel, its religion also has originated and developed, and how important elements of the Christian religion and the whole Western tradition have been built out of it. We have already encountered in the first beginnings of Israel's religion the fundamental recognition that history is the place where God acts, and this recognition is expressed especially in the stories of the patriarchs and in the tradition of the rescue from Egypt. In the story of God's covenant with Israel on Sinai we encountered the basic demands for human community life in this God-directed history. We saw then how, in the further course of its history, Israel was often faced with new questions and pushed forward with its faith in the one and only God into ever new areas. Above all, the area of nature was newly discovered and put in its proper place, although the relationship between religion and politics also became a crucial issue.

We have seen that the question was whether there were separate spheres of reality, with God competent to deal only in certain areas; and we have seen how in Israel, basically and with full consistency, the people maintained that there was only one all-encompassing reality and that the whole was under God's lordship. But we must also be very clear that

Israel and its leaders often went astray in practice and ran afoul of this principle, and that the prophets, to the contrary, had throughout the centuries led an impassioned battle to hold Israel to this its principle and to prevent it from being untrue to itself and thereby destroying itself. We saw, finally, how the same questions were reflected in the Psalms, which, being Israel's hymnal, offered us an insight into congregational worship and, at the same time, being Israel's prayer book, are an expression of the personal religion of the individual Israelite. Praise of God's faithfulness is the leading theme running through this personal religion and gives to the whole its inner cohesiveness.

The decisive thrust of Israelite religion is thus the consciousness that the people, and with it each individual, stands within a history that is directed by God according to his plan. Up to now, we have directed special attention to the fact that Israel understood its historical present on the basis of past events, that it lived on the basis of its history in recognizing the ground of the present in the past, and that it found therein standards for its life and activity in the present. But it has become evident more than once that historical thinking cannot be directed only to the past and the present, that the future belongs inseparably to it as well. For the essential nature of history lies in the fact that it has a beginning and an end, and that every event lies somewhere between these two end points. Not only what has passed, but also what is to come, is included in God's plan. For this reason, genuinely historical thinking is always directed toward the future.

Of course, a far-reaching distinction exists between the relationship to the past and the future. The event of the past lies open to the eyes, but the future is yet hidden; anyone can see what has already happened, but what is yet to occur evades our view. Nevertheless, it is not meaningless to speak of the future. For what will occur in the future is certainly not without connection with what has happened in the past. God does not act arbitrarily or disconnectedly, but according to a plan that includes the whole of history.

The question of plan and goal in God's activity is, from the very beginning, an essential part of Israelite historical thought. Turning back once more to the beginning of the tradition of Israel's history, we find that it says at the start of the story of the patriarchs: "Go from your country and your kindred and your father's house to the land that I will show you. And I will make of you a great nation, and I will bless you, and make your name great, so that you will be a blessing. . . . And in you all the families of the earth shall be blessed" (margin). We have already spoken of how certain important fundamentals of Israelite religion are expressed here: the promise of guidance and blessing and the consciousness of election. But when we now hold the forward-looking thrust of these words before our view, we must then consider the idea of the promise. What is expressed here is the promise to Abraham that he would become a great nation, that his nation would possess the Promised Land, and that the history of this nation would become a blessing for all mankind. The history that begins here is thus, by its very nature, quite decisively directed to the future. And that future is defined by a promise that pushes toward its fulfillment.

The fulfillment began. Israel became a nation and took possession of the land. This has been described at the conclusion of the long and tangled story that leads from the choice of Abraham to the final possession of the land by the Israelite tribes. In a speech in Josh. 23:14 it says: "You know in your hearts and souls, all of you, that not one thing has failed of all the good things which the LORD your God promised concerning you; all have come to pass for you, not one of them has failed." These sayings relate particularly to the promise of the land; it was wholly and completely fulfilled. But at the same time there yet remains at hand the greater, more inclusive content of the promise: that Israel will become a blessing for all nations. In the time of David also this promise was probably thought of as fulfilled. For, in the empire that David had created, many peoples were indeed united under the rule of Israel. But in its full sense the promise yet pointed beyond this limited political fulfillment. Indeed, we must say here that this fundamental promise at the beginning of Israel's history found its greatest fulfillment only after the time of the Old Testament. That Israel should become a blessing to all nations was fulfilled—but only in the fact that faith in the one, true God, which had its roots in Israel, came to all nations in the Christian religion.

Yet the promises are spoken of not only at the beginning of Israel's history. As time went on they came more clearly to the fore. It was, above all, the prophets who again and again announced a future act of God. We have already indicated that the prophet Nathan delivered the divine promise to King David. Primarily in Judah, where David's dynasty ruled after the separation of the two kingdoms of Israel and Judah, this promise played a major role. It had preserved the line of David undisputed for more than three centuries, and through it Judah was given a great inner stability. But the promise did not lose its power after the end of this state. The expectation that sometime there would yet come a king out of the line of David remained unshattered and vital: it is the expectation of the Messiah that has its roots here.

We have already encountered this expectation in the older prophets. It is expressed in familiar texts which have a firm place in Christian worship at Advent. Thus it reads in Isa., ch. 11:

There shall come forth a shoot from the stump of Jesse,
    and a branch shall grow out of his roots.
And the Spirit of the LORD shall rest upon him.

And the promise is found in Micah, ch. 5:

But you, O Bethlehem Ephrathah,
    who are little to be among the clans of Judah,
from you shall come forth for me
    one who is to be ruler in Israel,
whose origin is from of old,
    from ancient days.

It is clearly recognizable that these texts do not speak of an ordinary, earthly king. It is not only expected that one day a king, who will surpass all others, will sit on the throne of David in Jerusalem, but it is expected that God will make a wholly new beginning: This ruler will come forth out of the "stump" of Jesse; he will not constitute the crown of this mighty tree, but a new tree will develop out of the old root. The prophet Micah expresses the same thing when he says that this new king, this Messiah, will not simply mount the throne in Jerusalem, but that he will come forth yet again from Bethlehem, David's birthplace.

We must bear in mind that these words were spoken in a time when undisputed kings from the line of David sat on the throne in Jerusalem. The messianic promises of the prophets meant that the promise given to David was not fulfilled in the kings presently ruling; rather, it pointed far beyond them.

Here we see again the critical attitude of the prophets to their time. They could not accept much of what then existed and happened. They saw that Israel, and its kings in particular, had failed in the historical duties laid upon it. And they did not hesitate to draw inexorably the consequences of that failure. When Isaiah speaks of the stump of Jesse, he certainly means that the tree will first be cut down. Thus we then find, particularly in the prophets of the time of the collapse, in Jeremiah and Ezekiel, sharp words against the kings ruling in their time, combined with the proclamation of a new ruler from the line of David. Thus Jer., ch. 23, says: "Behold, the days are coming, says the LORD, when I will raise up for David a righteous Branch, and he shall reign as King and that wisely, and he shall execute justice and righteousness in the land. In his days Judah will be saved, and Israel will dwell securely. And this is the name by which he will be called: 'The LORD is our righteousness.' "

After the collapse of the Kingdom of Judah, this expectation of the Messiah remained alive; indeed, it constituted for the Jewish community of the following centuries an essential element of its future anticipation. We shall cite just one more prophetic word, characteristic of this late period, from Zech., ch. 9:

> Rejoice greatly, O daughter of Zion!
>   Shout aloud, O daughter of Jerusalem!
> Lo, your king comes to you;
>   triumphant and victorious is he,
> humble and riding on an ass,
>   on a colt the foal of an ass.
> I will cut off the chariot from Ephraim
>   and the war horse from Jerusalem;
> and the battle bow shall be cut off,
>   and he shall command peace to the nations;
> his dominion shall be from sea to sea,
>   and from the River to the ends of the earth.

There are two important ideas present in this message: The lordship of the Messiah will extend over the whole world, "from sea to sea and from the River to the ends of the earth" —indicating thereby the bounds of the then-known world. He is thus not only king over Israel, but over all nations. And the other: His kingdom will be one of perfect peace; all weapons will be destroyed and he himself will make peace among the nations by his word.

This promise remains unredeemed in the Old Testament. But Israel's history is by no means brought to an end with the Old Testament. For eventually, Jesus of Nazareth appeared in the midst of the people of Israel; in him the Christian community sees this messianic promise fulfilled. The fulfillment is, however, not yet final and conclusive. The Messiah is there, his rule over the nations has begun to come true—but his worldwide kingdom of peace has not yet appeared. Thus, out of this fulfillment also there is yet one more promise, one that aims at the final consummation.

But Israel's expectation and hope did not direct itself only to the Messiah. After the great collapse of the year 587 B.C., which meant the end of independent political history for

Israel, the nation's history itself became more and more the subject of hope. Israel had passed through the heights and the depths of history. It had experienced what it meant to live wholly in the consciousness of God's guidance—and what it meant to feel wholly abandoned by God. The two lie close together, for Israel had always passionately maintained that its historical experience was directly connected to God's activity. But that meant several things for the popular understanding: When things went well for Israel, God did it; when they went badly, he had thus abandoned the nation. The old traditions of God's great historical acts of salvation were often the measure by which alone the present history was measured.

But already, in the dark days when the Kingdom of Judah perished, Jeremiah had energetically declared these alternatives to be false. Simply to look backward to the great times of salvation history will not suffice for the present with its historical duties. Even the present trouble must be understood as God's doing, as a judgment on his people. But Jeremiah had previously come to understand that the present received its full meaning only in connection with the future yet standing before it.

A few centuries later, an anonymous prophet, whose words come to us in chs. 40 to 55 of Isaiah (scholars call him "Deutero-Isaiah," the second Isaiah), carried out this turning to the future with complete consistency. He lived among the captive Judeans in Babylon. Several decades had passed since the destruction of Judah, and among the captives hopelessness and resignation spread more and more. They lived wholly in the memory of the old traditions from the past great period of their nation's history. But precisely against this background their own present situation must have appeared the more unbearable. "The LORD has forsaken me, my Lord has forgotten me"—such was the general attitude.

And voices were also raised, asking whether it was so certain that the God of Israel was the only and true God, whether the gods of the Babylonians had not shown themselves to be the stronger because they had granted victory to their nation and because Israel's God obviously could do nothing more for his people. These were difficult and dangerous questions. If the captives gave themselves over to this thinking and opened themselves to the Babylonian religion, it would lead inevitably to their sooner or later disappearing into the local population and thus their ceasing to have any part in God's dealings with Israel.

Here it becomes clear once again how the existence of the nation, or at any rate the captive part of the nation, would stand or fall with its faith in the one God who had revealed himself as the God of Israel. It was the one thing that held the captive Judeans together and could protect them from merging into their surroundings.

Into their situation came the prophet whom we call Deutero-Isaiah. His words are the most beautiful and impressive that one can find in the Old Testament. They are impregnated with a passionate appeal to a people captive and filled with hopelessness and doubt, and, at the same time, carry on a vehement battle for the honor and uniqueness of Israel's God. "Comfort, comfort my people, says your God"—with these words begins the proclamation of Deutero-Isaiah as we have received it. In ever new words he comforts the weary and hopeless:

> Why do you say, O Jacob,
>   and speak, O Israel,
> "My way is hid from the LORD,
>   and my right is disregarded by my God"?
> Have you not known? Have you not heard?
> The LORD is the everlasting God,
>   the Creator of the ends of the earth.
> He does not faint or grow weary,
>
> . . . .
>
> but they who wait for the LORD shall renew
>   their strength,
>   they shall mount up with wings like eagles,

they shall run and not be weary,
they shall walk and not faint.

But it is not cheap comfort which the prophet gives here. He
does not demand of his captive fellow countrymen that they
believe what he says without examination. He reminds them
again and again of what they themselves have known from
childhood and what their ancestors had experienced as true,
over the centuries. In the words just quoted it can be heard:
"Have you not known? Have you not heard?" Again and again
the prophet calls to memory the whole body of the ancient
tradition of the story of salvation, and above all he quotes
again and again to the captives out of the songs of worship,
the Psalms, in order to remind them of what they themselves
and their fathers had always known. And, as do the Psalms,
he extends his view as far as the creation:

The LORD is the everlasting God,
the Creator of the ends of the earth

The crucial factor is that the prophet does not stop with this
backward look, but resolutely draws his conclusions from it.
On the one hand he turns to those who were beginning to
doubt the power of Israel's God. He puts all this before their
view and asks them: Where is there a God who could be compared with this one? Who created heaven and earth? Who directs the course of the stars? Who has already announced every happening through his prophets and then caused it to take
place? This is passionate and embattled talk that the prophet
engages in with his fellow captives; indeed, they often take
on the form of outright legal proceedings. He challenges
the gods of the other nations to appear in a lawsuit and to
prove that they are gods at all. He directs shockingly bold and
passionate attacks against the other gods and against those
who would rely on them. And he derives an unruffled certainty, which speaks out of his words, from the deep and
broad stream of the centuries-old tradition of his people.
But this defense is only one side of his proclamation. The

other is wholly and completely positive. Out of the tradition
of the power and uniqueness of God, the prophet derives the
certainty that God's action toward his people is not yet at an
end, indeed, that the decisive act is yet to come. For that reason he employs all his power and passion to direct the view
of the people toward the future. He announces to the captives
that the time of their bondage is at an end:

> Comfort, comfort my people,
>   says your God.
> Speak tenderly to Jerusalem,
>   and cry to her
> that her warfare is ended,
>   that her iniquity is pardoned.

And he portrays how God will lead them out of captivity back
to the land in a vast, wonderful march through the desert, in
which God himself leads the way:

> A voice cries:
> "In the wilderness prepare the way of the LORD,
>   make straight in the desert a highway for our God.
> Every valley shall be lifted up,
>   and every mountain and hill be made low;
> the uneven ground shall become level,
>   and the rough places a plain.
> And the glory of the LORD shall be revealed,
>   and all flesh shall see it together,
>   for the mouth of the LORD has spoken."

This forthcoming act of God is the only thing that matters
now. We have seen how deeply the prophet is rooted in the
tradition of his people; but in spite of this he can challenge
the captive Judeans:

> Remember not the former things,
>   nor consider the things of old.
> Behold, I am doing a new thing;
>   now it springs forth, do you not perceive it?

Looking at the past alone is not enough; indeed, that can completely prevent the recognition of what is now happening. It

is therefore necessary to be wholly open to this new event.

The view of the prophet is directed forward so firmly that everything else must take a back seat. It must have appeared to the godly among the captive Judeans as near blasphemy when he challenged them to stop thinking about earlier events and no longer to consider the past. And that meant to disregard the ancient, sanctified traditions about God's great acts of salvation! This meant an attack on the foundations of the religious and national existence of Israel!

Yet the prophet by no means intends a devaluation of the ancient traditions. Again and again he had directed the attention of his hearers to the fulfillment of God's promises in Israel's history. But it was no longer a time for looking back; now God intended to create something new, now he intended a new era in Israel's history to begin. Therefore it was now necessary to look forward and be prepared for this act of God.

The life of Israel could begin anew once more. When the Persians destroyed the Babylonian Empire, they permitted the Judeans to rebuild the Temple in Jerusalem, and gradually the greater part of the exiles returned to the land of their fathers. They did not make here any glorious new beginning, and there yet remained segments of the people in the Dispersion in Babylonia, in Egypt, and in other lands of the Near East. In Jerusalem itself the Temple formed a focal point, and here a new religious life developed under the leadership of the priesthood, a life controlled by stringent rules. During this period the Law acquired its great significance for the Jewish people. But at the same time this new element persisted and was never again lost—the knowledge that God will again act in the future, that something new is ever imminent, that his plan has not yet come anywhere near its final goal.

Israel's faith remained pointed toward the future from then on. Indeed, the expectation of a future act of God became even stronger in the following centuries. And there became evident more and more what was already observable in the proclamation of Deutero-Isaiah, that this expectation concerned the destiny not only of Israel but of the whole world.

God's work of salvation had begun in Israel, the history of this nation had been chosen by God to form the basis for his action in the entire world. And this inclusive new act of God was now imminent and became ever more passionately awaited. It was, however, at the same time expected as the final and conclusive act of God in the world and thus as the end of history. And this end of history itself must be, in an ultimate sense, an act of the God who had said of himself, "I am the first and I am the last; besides me there is no god" (Isa. 44:6).

The perception that history has an end has ever since been an inalienable element in the Israelite-Christian understanding of the world and history. In the course of the centuries it has taken the most varied forms. Much of it, including that which occurs in the Biblical writings, strikes us today as very strange and can scarcely serve any longer to express our understanding of the end of history. Our general situation today does not allow us to express this insight in such definite, concretely out-lined presentations. Nevertheless, without this insight we shall not obtain a sufficient understanding of history.

This is by no means only a question for theologians and philosophers but a basic issue of the historical existence of each individual. For, the fact that history has an end means not only that it will cease some time or other but primarily that it has a goal. Only on the basis of this goal can we under-stand the final end of our own history.

But is there not a deep contradiction here? How should we stand our own history on the basis of history's end, which has yet to come? In this question all the lines with which we have attempted to sketch the history and the understanding of history from the Old Testament converge as it were yet one more time.

The end of history is yet not simply the great unknown. It is the end of that history which has been encountered for thousands of years as God's history, which is defined by his election and his promises, which includes the whole indivisible reality, and which has its inner cohesiveness in God's faithfulness to himself and his promises, even through judgment. That God has set a goal for this history means, however, nothing other than that he will bring to a conclusion all that he has begun in it, and that he will put an end to all that opposes this conclusion. The end of history will be God's full and final yes to this history. To understand history from its end thus means to trust the future action of God in its final result. It means basing one's particular historical existence wholly on this confidence. This does not mean flight out of the present in expectation of a better future. But the present, in which it is our duty to live responsibly, receives through this its place in the great movement of history toward its goal. The present is not the ultimate; the meaning of our life and our history will not be decided in it, but it is a point along the way toward the fulfillment and completion of history.

Thus our historical existence is grounded in confidence in the faithfulness of God, who is the first and the last, and who has established the beginning and the goal of history. Israel has abundantly experienced this faithfulness and, even in the dark depths of its history, maintained its confidence in it. Indeed, precisely in those depths must this confidence prove true and show its sustaining power.

We stand again today in such a time of trial. Even for us confidence in God's faithfulness is rooted in the various historical experiences of Israel. But in regard to basic historical experience we are richer than the men of the Old Testament. In the resurrection of Jesus, God has spoken his yes to this history and thereby confirmed beforehand our expectations and hopes. We are still on the way, for the end of history has not yet come. But our faith, our confidence in the future, rests on this yes of God, who is the first and the last.